COSORI AIR FRYER COOKBOOK

The Ultimate Air Fryer Recipes with Beginner's Guide For Your COSORI Air Fryer

By Lisa Cook

Copyright ©2019 By Lisa Cook

All rights reserved.

No part of this guide may be reproduced in any form without permission in writing from the publisher except in the case of brief quotations embodied in critical articles or reviews.

Legal & Disclaimer

The information contained in this book and its contents is not designed to replace or take the place of any form of medical or professional advice; and is not meant to replace the need for independent medical, financial, legal or other professional advice or services, as may be required. The content and information in this book has been provided for educational and entertainment purposes only.

The content and information contained in this book has been compiled from sources deemed reliable, and it is accurate to the best of the Author's knowledge, information and belief. However, the Author cannot guarantee its accuracy and validity and cannot be held liable for any errors and/or omissions. Further, changes are periodically made to this book as and when needed. Where appropriate and/or necessary, you must consult a professional (including but not limited to your doctor, attorney, financial advisor or such other professional advisor) before using any of the suggested remedies, techniques, or information in this book.

Upon using the contents and information contained in this book, you agree to hold harmless the Author from and against any damages, costs, and expenses, including any legal fees potentially resulting from the application of any of the information provided by this book. This disclaimer applies to any loss, damages or injury caused by the use and application, whether directly or indirectly, of any advice or information presented, whether for breach of contract, tort, negligence, personal injury, criminal intent, or under any other cause of action.

Table of contents

Chapter 1 Beginner's Guide to COSORI Air Fryer ... 1
COSORI Air Fryer Features ... 2
How to Use Your Air Fryer? ... 3
Air Fryer Cleaning and Maintenance ... 4
Benefits of COSORI Air Fryer ... 6

Chapter 2 Breakfast and Brunch ... 7
Cheesy Bread ... 7
Leek and Potato Frittata ... 8
Ham Pie ... 9
Cinnamon Toast ... 10
Tasty Scrambled Eggs ... 11
Breakfast Cherries Risotto ... 12
Veggie Burritos Breakfast ... 13
Potato Hash ... 14
Veggie Mix ... 15
Special Corn Flakes Casserole ... 16
Broccoli Quiches ... 17
Spinach Parcels ... 18
Breakfast Shrimp Frittata ... 19

Chapter 3 Appetizers and Sides ... 20
Salsa Black Bean Salad ... 20
Easy Onion and Corn Spread ... 21
Artichoke Spread ... 22
Olives and Eggplant Dip ... 23
Veggie Cakes ... 24
Tomatoes Salsa ... 26

Chard Party Spread	27
Tomato and Bell Pepper Dip	28
Corn Side Salad	29
Colored Veggie Mix	30
Leeks Medley	31
Corn and Tomatoes	32

Chapter4 Poultry 33

Turkey and Parsley Pesto	33
Chicken Breasts and Veggies	34
Chicken and Green Coconut Sauce	35
Simple Chicken Thighs	36
Chicken Breasts Delight	37
Tomato Chicken Mix	38
Chicken and Veggies	39
Japanese Chicken Thighs	40
Air Fried Whole Chicken	41
Chicken Thighs and Rice	42

Chapter5 Beef, Pork and Lamb 43

Beef Rolls	43
Greek Beef Meatballs Salad	44
Beef Patties and Mushroom Sauce	46
Beef Casserole	48
Lamb and Spinach Mix	49
Lamb and Lemon Sauce	51
Lamb and Green Pesto	52
Lamb and Lemon Sauce Recipe	53
Provencal Pork Recipe	54
Lemony Lamb Leg Recipe	55

  Beef Roast and Wine Sauce Recipe 56

  Fennel Flavored Pork Roast Recipe 57

  Stuffed Pork Steaks 58

  Pork Chops and Mushrooms Mix 60

  Beef Stuffed Squash 61

Chapter6 Vegan and Vegetarian 63

  Cajun Asparagus 63

  Squash Salad 64

  Creamy Squash Mix 65

  Orange Carrots 66

  Tomato Salad 67

  Tomato and Green Beans Salad 68

  Bell Peppers and Kale 69

  Garlic Parsnips 70

  Broccoli and Pomegranate 71

  Bacon Cauliflower 72

Chapter7 Desserts 73

  Crispy Apples Recipe 73

  Chocolate Cookies Recipe 74

  Lentils and Dates Brownies Recipe 75

  Strawberry Shortcakes Recipe 76

  Cocoa Cookies Recipe 78

  Mini Lava Cakes Recipe 79

  Lime Cheesecake Recipe 80

  Plum Cake Recipe 81

  Ginger Cheesecake Recipe 82

  Cocoa and Almond Bars Recipe 83

Conclusion 84

Chapter1 Beginner's Guide to COSORI Air Fryer

With the growing demand for healthier cooking and better nutrition, people have turned to the air fryer as an alternative way of cooking without fat. After all, too much fat from fried foods in one's diet contributes to obesity and cardiovascular diseases. However, fat really does make food palatable. No wonder it's tough to give up that pleasant fried taste.

With an air fryer, though, you capture the great taste of fried foods without the use of oil. It's a practical way for anyone striving to become slim and healthy. Now, I'd like to introduce one of the most popular brand Air Fryer-COSORI.

COSORI Air Fryer Features

Why I would like to introduce the air fryer of this brand? It is because I have used this air fryer for 3 months. Its many features and advantages have brought me great convenience and fun. Those features will make you love it better.

Highly Portable:
Designed to easily be transferred from your kitchen storage cabinet to the countertop or to and from any place in your home – making it great to take to a friend for a cook-off

Cooking Presets:
This is the silver bullet of air fryers repertoire as it completely eliminates the need to set cooking times and temperatures for your commonly cooked foods. Ingredient specifications are preprogrammed into the appliance an all you have to do is choose the correct one, and with the push of a button the preset has got you covered

Digital Touch Screen:
No need to have to learn about complicated cooking maneuvers or have master culinary skills to use your air fryer. Simplicity is inbuilt with this feature. Most models allow you to set your cooking preferences with just a few taps on the touch panel's screen and voila, you are good to go

Automatic Temperature control:
Get a perfectly cooked food every time. Just set your air fryer to your desired temperature and you can be assured that it will effortlessly cook your food to the desired doneness

Timer and buzzer:
No need to worry about having to constantly keep an eye on your food or about accidentally overcooking it. With this feature, you are frequently given audio cues on the progress of your meal

How to Use Your Air Fryer?

This appliance comes with a manual for easy assembly and as a handy guide for first-time users. Most brands also include a pamphlet of recipes to give you ideas about the wide range of dishes that you can create using this single kitchen appliance. Once you are ready to cook and you have all your ingredients ready, put them in the basket and insert it into the fryer. Other recipes will require you to preheat the air fryer before using. Once the basket is in, set the temperature and timer and begin cooking.

You can use an air fryer to cook food in a variety of ways. Once you get used with the basics, you can try its other features, such as advanced baking and using air fryer dehydrators.

Here are some of the cooking techniques that you can do with this single appliance:

- **Fry:** You can actually omit oil in cooking but a little amount adds crunch and flavor to your food. You can add oil to the ingredients while mixing or lightly spray the food with oil before cooking. You can use most kinds of oils but many users prefer peanut, olive, sunflower, and canola oils.
- **Roast:** You can produce the same quality of roasted foods like the ones cooked in a conventional roaster in a faster manner. This is recommended to people who need to come up with a special dish but do not have much time to prepare.
- **Bake:** There are baking pans suited for this appliance that you can use to bake bread, cookies, and other pastries. It only takes around 15 to 30 minutes to get your baked goodies done.
- **Grill:** It effectively grills your food easily and without mess. You only need to shake the basket halfway through the cooking process or flip the ingredients once or twice depending on the instructions. To make it easier, you can put the ingredients in a grill pan or grill layer with a handle, which other models include in the package or you can also buy one as an added accessory.

There are many kinds of foods that you can cook using an air fryer, but there are also certain types that are not suited for it. Avoid cooking ingredients, which can be steamed, like beans and carrots. You also cannot fry foods covered in heavy batter in this appliance.

Aside from the above mentioned, you can cook most kinds of ingredients using an air fryer. You can use it to cook foods covered in light flour or bread crumbs. You can cook a variety of vegetables in the appliance, such as cauliflower, asparagus, zucchini, kale, peppers, and corn on the cob. You can also use it to cook frozen foods and home prepared meals by following a different set of instructions for these purposes.

An air fryer also comes with another useful feature - the separator. It allows you to cook multiple dishes at a time. Use the separator to divide ingredients in the pan or basket. You have to make sure that all ingredients have the same temperature setting so that everything will cook evenly at the same time.

Air Fryer Cleaning and Maintenance

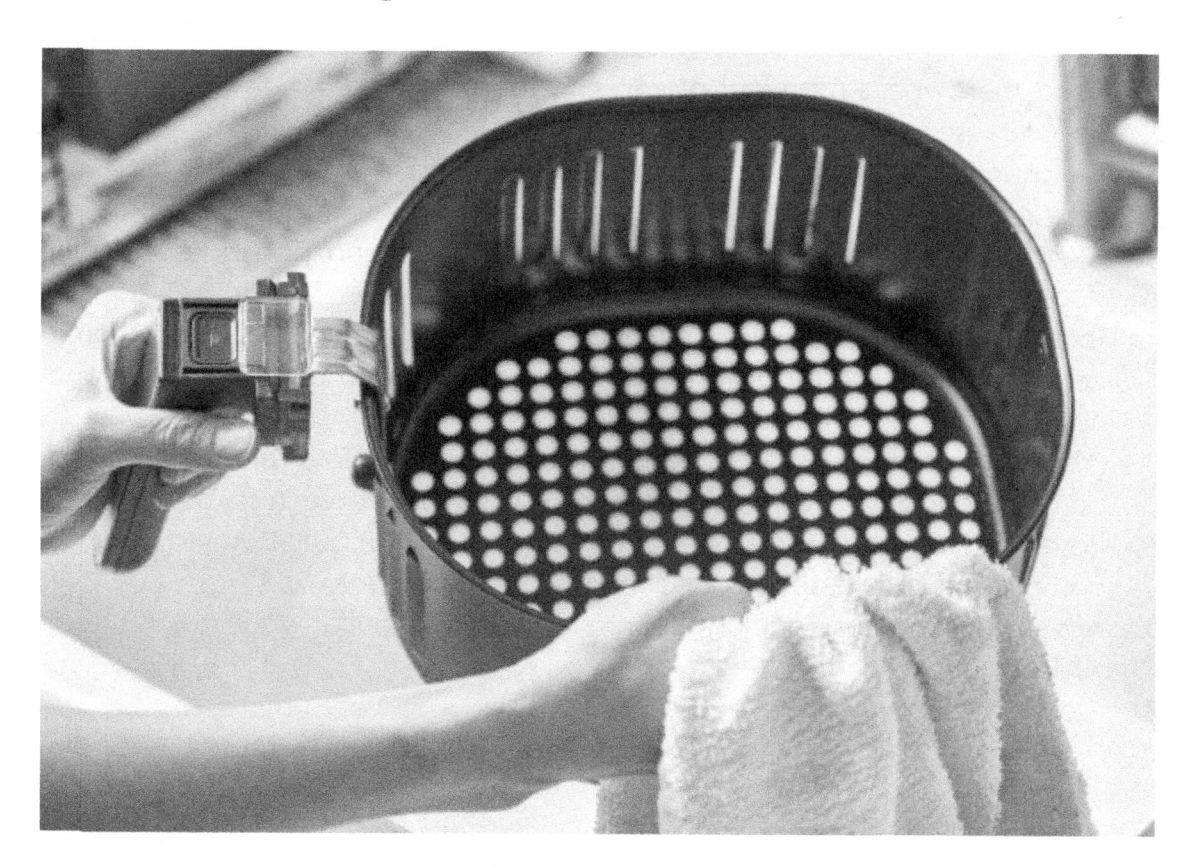

Cleaning COSORI air fryer is easy and it does not require you to do a lot of complicated tasks. The first thing that you need to do is to unplug the air fryer before cleaning to prevent electrocution. The basket is dishwasher-friendly, so you can take it out from the fryer's chamber and clean them in the sink or in the dishwasher.

Once you remove the fryer basket, give extra attention to the base of the fryer where most of the drippings from the food have collected and dried. Make sure that you remove the browning that has accumulated at the base as this can lead to burning in future cooking. You can remove the browning by spraying it with warm soapy water and allowing it to soak for at least an hour. This will soften the browning, so you can easily wipe it clean.

Aside from taking care of the inside of the air fryer, it is also important to clean the exterior using a warm moist cloth.

General maintenance should be undertaken regularly to keep the air-fryer in optimal condition:

1. Read the owner's manual before using the air-fryer or when in any doubt about its use.
2. The air-fryer must always be upright on a level surface when in use.
3. Be sure that the air-fryer is clean and free of deposits and dust before use. Clean out the interior and make sure the basket and pan is free of any stubborn food residue.
4. To ensure the air-fryer is not at risk of overheating, it should be at least 10cm's from the wall or other appliances in every direction, to allow for steam and hot air to escape while in use.
5. Properly inspect the cords, basket, pan and handle before use. Cords should be clean and intact, as a compromised plug could cause injury or fatality. A frayed or faulty plug should never be inserted into an outlet. Any damaged components should be replaced through the manufacturer.
6. Never have the air-fryer plugged into an electrical outlet when not in use or while stored.
7. Clean the air-fryer after every use.

Benefits of COSORI Air Fryer

Besides providing us comfort and satisfaction, eating fried foods provide little benefits. But with COSORI air fryer, anyone can whip up healthy and satisfying foods minus any guilt. There are many benefits of air frying your food instead of cooking them in a conventional deep fryer. Below are the benefits of why you should air fry your foods more often.

- **Versatile:** An air fryer is not only a fryer thus you can use it to cook different types of foods. You can use it to bake bread, make popcorn or even make roasted vegetables.
- **Cost effective:** Since you don't use any oil in cooking your food, you can save a lot of money from buying cooking oil.
- **Easy to cook:** Never mind if you are a kitchen novice. Since air fryers are digital, it requires less skill so you can cook delicious dishes even if you are not good at cooking.
- **Fewer calories**: Since you do not add any oil to cook your food compared to traditional frying methods, you don't add a few calories to cook your food. Remember that a cup of oil is already equivalent to 800 calories alone so deep frying increases the caloric value of your food to a dangerously high level.

The thing is that there are many benefits of air frying and if you decide to make a simple change in your diet by only eating fried foods that are cooked in an air fryer, you will be able to enjoy a healthier and more convenient life.

Chapter 2 Breakfast and Brunch

Cheesy Bread

Preparation time: 18 Minutes
Servings: 3

Ingredients:
- 6 bread slices
- 5 tbsp. butter; melted
- 3 garlic cloves; minced
- 6 tsp. sun dried tomato pesto
- 1 cup mozzarella cheese; grated

Directions:
1. Cut the prepared bread into small pieces, arrange butter on one side of bread.
2. Whisk together the tomato sauce, garlic and cheese in a bowl. Spread evenly over the bread
3. Add bread slices to your heated air fryer and cook them at 350 °F, for 8 minutes. Divide among plates and serve for breakfast.

Nutrition:
Calories: 187; Fat: 5; Fiber: 6; Carbs: 8; Protein: 3

Leek and Potato Frittata

Preparation time: 28 Minutes
Servings: 4

Ingredients:
- 2 gold potatoes; boiled, peeled and chopped.
- 1/4 cup whole milk
- 10 eggs; whisked
- 5 oz. fromage blanc; crumbled
- 2 tbsp. butter
- 2 leeks; sliced
- Salt and black pepper to the taste

Directions:
1. Heat up a pan that fits your air fryer with the butter over medium heat, add leeks; stir and cook for 4 minutes.
2. Add potatoes, salt, pepper, eggs, cheese and milk, whisk well; cook for 1 minute more, introduce in your air fryer and cook at 350 °F, for 13 minutes. Slice frittata, divide among plates and serve.

Nutrition:
Calories: 271; Fat: 6; Fiber: 8; Carbs: 12; Protein: 6

Ham Pie

Preparation time: 35 Minutes
Servings: 6

Ingredients:
- 16 oz. crescent rolls dough
- 1 tbsp. parmesan; grated
- 2 cups ham; cooked and chopped.
- 2 eggs; whisked
- 2 cups cheddar cheese; grated
- Salt and black pepper to the taste
- Cooking spray

Directions:
1. Use a knife to cut half a crescent of bread incompletely in the middle.
2. In a bowl; mix eggs with cheddar cheese, parmesan, salt and pepper; whisk well and add into the dough.
3. Spread ham, cut them into strips, then arrange them between the crescent rolls dough.
4. Grease your air fryer's pan with cooking spray and put the crescent rolls dough on the bottom.
5. Cook at 300 °F, for 25 minutes. Slice pie and serve for breakfast.

Nutrition:
Calories: 400; Fat: 27; Fiber: 7; Carbs: 22; Protein: 16

Cinnamon Toast

Preparation time: 15 Minutes
Servings: 6

Ingredients:

- 1 stick butter; soft
- 12 bread slices
- 1 ½ tsp. vanilla extract
- 1 ½ tsp. cinnamon powder
- 1/2 cup sugar

Directions:

1. In a bowl; mix soft butter with sugar, vanilla and cinnamon and whisk well.
2. Spread this on bread slices; place them in your air fryer and cook at 400 °F, for 5 minutes; divide among plates and serve for breakfast.

Nutrition:

Calories: 221; Fat: 4; Fiber: 7; Carbs: 12; Protein: 8

Tasty Scrambled Eggs

Preparation time: 20 Minutes
Servings: 2

Ingredients:
- 2 eggs
- 2 tbsp. butter
- 1 green bell pepper; chopped.
- 1 red bell pepper; chopped
- 1 fresh chives
- Salt and black pepper to the taste
- A pinch of sweet paprika

Directions:
1. In a bowl; mix eggs with salt, pepper, chives, paprika and green/red bell pepper and whisk well.
2. Heat up your air fryer at 140 degrees F; add butter and melt it.
3. Add eggs mix; stir and cook for 10 minutes. Divide scrambled eggs on plates and serve for breakfast.

Nutrition:
Calories: 200; Fat: 4; Fiber: 7; Carbs: 10; Protein: 3

Breakfast Cherries Risotto

Preparation time: 22 Minutes
Servings: 4

Ingredients:
- 8 cups Arborio rice, cooked
- 1 ½ tsp. cinnamon powder
- 1 cup corn kernels
- 3/4 cup of peas
- 1 cup apple juice
- 3 cups milk
- 1/2 cup cherries; dried
- 1/3 cup brown sugar
- A pinch of salt
- 2 tbsp. butter

Directions:
1. Heat up your air fryer pan with the butter over medium heat, add the rice, stir and cook for 4-5 minutes.
2. Add sugar, corn kernels, peas, apple juice, milk, cinnamon and cherries; stir, introduce in your air fryer and cook at 350 °F, for 8 minutes. Divide into bowls and serve for breakfast.

Nutrition:
Calories: 162; Fat: 12; Fiber: 6; Carbs: 23; Protein: 8

Veggie Burritos Breakfast

Preparation time: 20 Minutes
Servings: 4

Ingredients:

- 1/2 cup sweet potatoes; steamed and cubed
- 1/2 small broccoli head; florets separated and steamed
- 2 tbsp. cashew butter
- 2 tbsp. tamari
- 2 tbsp. water
- 2 tbsp. liquid smoke
- 4 rice papers
- 7 asparagus stalks
- 8 roasted red peppers; chopped
- A handful kale; chopped

Directions:

1. In a bowl; mix cashew butter with water, tamari and liquid smoke and whisk well.
2. Wet rice papers and arrange them on a working surface.
3. Divide sweet potatoes, broccoli, asparagus, red peppers and kale; wrap burritos and dip each in cashew mix.
4. Arrange burritos in your air fryer and cook them at 350 °F, for 10 minutes. Divide veggie burritos on plates d serve.

Nutrition:

Calories: 172; Fat: 4; Fiber: 7; Carbs: 8; Protein: 3

Potato Omelet

Preparation time: 35 Minutes
Servings: 4

Ingredients:

- 1 ½ potatoes; cubed
- 1 yellow onion; chopped.
- 2 tsp. olive oil
- 2 eggs
- 1/2 tsp. thyme; dried
- 1 green bell pepper; chopped
- Salt and black pepper to the taste

Directions:

1. Heat up your air fryer at 350 degrees F; add oil, heat it up, add onion, bell pepper, salt and pepper; stir and cook for 5 minutes.
2. Add potatoes, thyme and eggs, stir, cover and cook at 360 °F, for 20 minutes. Divide among plates and serve for breakfast.

Nutrition:

Calories: 241; Fat: 4; Fiber: 7; Carbs: 12; Protein: 7

Veggie Mix

Preparation time: 35 Minutes
Servings: 6

Ingredients:
- 1 yellow onion; sliced
- 1 red bell pepper; chopped.
- 1 gold potato; chopped.
- 2 tbsp. olive oil
- 8 eggs
- 2 tbsp. mustard
- 3 cups milk
- 8 oz. brie; trimmed and cubed
- 12 oz. sourdough bread; cubed
- 4 oz. parmesan; grated
- Salt and black pepper to the taste

Directions:
1. Heat up your air fryer at 350 degrees F; add oil, onion, potato and bell pepper and cook for 5 minutes.
2. In a bowl; mix eggs with milk, salt, pepper and mustard and whisk well.
3. Add bread and brie to your air fryer; Add the vegetables and seasoning mixture.
4. Add the rest of the bread and parmesan; toss just a little bit and cook for 20 minutes.
5. Divide among plates and serve for breakfast.

Nutrition:
Calories: 231; Fat: 5; Fiber: 10; Carbs: 20; Protein: 12

Special Corn Flakes Casserole

Preparation time: 18 Minutes
Servings: 5

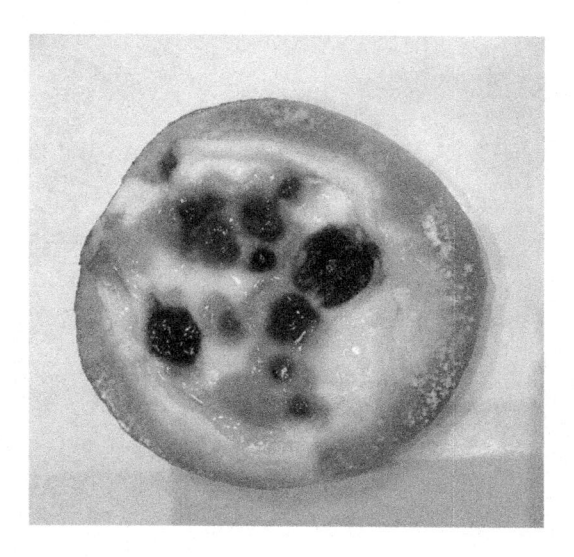

Ingredients:
- 1/3 cup milk
- 4 tbsp. cream cheese; whipped
- 1/4 tsp. nutmeg; ground
- 1/4 cup blueberries
- 1 ½ cups corn flakes; crumbled
- 3 tsp. sugar
- 2 eggs; whisked
- 5 bread slices

Directions:
1. In a bowl; mix eggs with sugar, nutmeg and milk and whisk well.
2. In another bowl; mix cream cheese with blueberries and whisk well.
3. Put corn flakes in a third bowl.
4. Spread blueberry mix on each bread slice; then dip in eggs mix and dredge in corn flakes at the end.
5. Place bread in your air fryer's basket; heat up at 400 °F and bake for 8 minutes. Divide among plates and serve for breakfast.

Nutrition:
Calories: 300; Fat: 5; Fiber: 7; Carbs: 16; Protein: 4

Broccoli Quiches

Preparation time: 30 Minutes
Servings: 2

Ingredients:
- 1 broccoli head; florets separated and steamed
- 1 tomato; chopped.
- 1 tsp. thyme; chopped
- 1 carrots; chopped and steamed
- 2 oz. cheddar cheese; grated
- 2 oz. milk
- 1 tsp. parsley; chopped
- 2 eggs
- Salt and black pepper to the taste

Directions:
1. In a bowl; mix eggs with milk, parsley, thyme, salt and pepper and whisk well.
2. Put broccoli, carrots and tomato in your air fryer.
3. Add eggs mix on top, spread cheddar cheese; cover and cook at 350 °F, for 20 minutes. Divide among plates and serve for breakfast.

Nutrition:
Calories: 214; Fat: 4; Fiber: 7; Carbs: 12; Protein: 3

Spinach Parcels

Preparation time: 14 Minutes
Servings: 2

Ingredients:
- 1 lb. baby spinach leaves; roughly chopped
- 4 sheets filo pastry
- 1/2 lb. ricotta cheese
- 2 tbsp. pine nuts
- 1 eggs; whisked
- Zest from 1 lemon; grated
- Greek yogurt for serving
- Salt and black pepper to the taste

Directions:
1. In a bowl; mix spinach with cheese, egg, lemon zest, salt, pepper and pine nuts and stir.
2. Arrange filo sheets on a working surface, divide spinach mix; fold diagonally to shape your parcels and place them in your preheated air fryer at 400 degrees F. Bake parcels for 4 minutes; divide them on plates and serve them with Greek yogurt on the side.

Nutrition:
Calories: 182; Fat: 4; Fiber: 8; Carbs: 9; Protein: 5

Breakfast Shrimp Frittata

Preparation time: 25 Minutes
Servings: 4

Ingredients:

- 4 eggs
- 1/2 cup shrimp; cooked, peeled, deveined and chopped.
- 1/2 cup baby spinach; chopped.
- 1/2 tsp. basil; dried
- Cooking spray
- Salt and black pepper to the taste
- 1/2 cup rice; cooked
- 1/2 cup Monterey jack cheese; grated

Directions:

1. In a bowl; mix eggs with salt, pepper and basil and whisk.
2. Grease your air fryer's pan with cooking spray and add rice, shrimp and spinach.
3. Add eggs mix, sprinkle cheese all over and cook in your air fryer at 350 °F, for 10 minutes. Divide among plates and serve for breakfast.

Nutrition:

Calories: 162; Fat: 6; Fiber: 5; Carbs: 8; Protein: 4

Chapter3 Appetizers and Sides

Salsa Black Bean Salad

Preparation time: 10 minutes
Cooking time: 20 minutes
Servings: 7

Ingredients:
- 1 tablespoon coconut aminos
- ½ teaspoon cumin, ground
- 1 cup canned black beans, drained
- 1 cup salsa
- 6 cups romaine lettuce leaves
- ½ cup avocado, peeled, pitted and mashed

Directions:
1. In a pan that fits your air fryer, mix black beans with salsa, cumin and aminos, stir, put in the fryer and cook at 350 degrees F for 20 minutes.
2. In a salad bowl, mix lettuce leaves with black beans mix and mashed avocado, toss and serve as an appetizer.
3. Enjoy!

Nutrition:
calories 231, fat 4, fiber 7, carbs 15, protein 3

Easy Onion and Corn Spread

Preparation time: 10 minutes
Cooking time: 15 minutes
Servings: 8

Ingredients:
- 30 ounces canned corn, drained
- 2 green onions, chopped
- ½ cup coconut cream
- 8 ounces tofu, crumbled
- 1 jalapeno, chopped
- ½ teaspoon chili powder

Directions:
1. In a pan that fits your air fryer, mix corn with green onions, coconut cream, tofu, chili powder and jalapeno, stir, transfer to your fryer and cook at 350 degrees F for 15 minutes.
2. Divide into bowls and serve as a dip.
3. Enjoy!

Nutrition:
calories 252, fat 5, fiber 10, carbs 17, protein 4

Artichoke Spread

Preparation time: 10 minutes
Cooking time: 20 minutes
Servings: 8

Ingredients:
- 28 ounces canned artichokes, drained and chopped
- 10 ounces spinach
- 8 ounces coconut cream
- 1 yellow onion, chopped
- 2 garlic cloves, minced
- ¾ cup coconut milk
- ½ cup tofu, pressed and crumbled
- 1/3 cup vegan avocado mayonnaise
- 1 tablespoon red vinegar
- A pinch of salt and black pepper

Directions:
1. In a pan that fits your air fryer, mix artichokes with spinach, coconut cream, onion, garlic, coconut milk, tofu, avocado mayo, vinegar, salt and pepper, stir well, introduce in the fryer and cook at 365 degrees F for 20 minutes.
2. Divide into bowls and serve as an appetizer.
3. Enjoy!

Nutrition:
calories 215, fat 4, fiber 4, carbs 19, protein 13

Olives and Eggplant Dip

Preparation time: 10 minutes
Cooking time: 10 minutes
Servings: 6

Ingredients:

- 2 pounds eggplant, sliced
- Salt and black pepper to the taste
- 1 tablespoon olive oil
- 4 garlic cloves, chopped
- ½ cup water
- Juice of 1 lemon
- ¼ cup black olives, pitted
- 1 tablespoon sesame paste
- 4 thyme springs, chopped

Directions:

1. In a pan that fits your air fryer, combine oil with eggplants, salt, pepper, garlic, water, lemon juice, olives and thyme, stir, introduce in your fryer and cook at 370 degrees F for 10 minutes.
2. Blend your dip with an immersion blender, add sesame paste, blend again, divide into bowls and serve.
3. Enjoy!

Nutrition:
calories 205, fat 11, fiber 4, carbs 14, protein 2

Veggie Cakes

Preparation time: 10 minutes
Cooking time: 20 minutes
Servings: 8

Ingredients:
- 2 teaspoons ginger, grated
- 1 cup yellow onion, chopped
- 1 cup mushrooms, minced
- 1 cup canned red lentils, drained
- ¼ cup veggie stock
- 1 sweet potato, chopped
- ¼ cup parsley, chopped
- ¼ cup hemp seeds
- 1 tablespoon curry powder
- ¼ cup cilantro, chopped
- A drizzle of olive oil
- 1 cup quick oats
- 2 tablespoons rice flour

Directions:
1. Heat up a pan with the oil over medium-high heat, add ginger, onion and mushrooms, stir and cook for 2-3 minutes.
2. Add lentils, potato and stock, stir, cook for 5-6 minutes, take off heat, cool the whole mixture and mash it with a fork.
3. Add parsley, cilantro, hemp, oats, curry powder and rice flour, stir well and shape medium cakes out of this mix.

4. Place veggie cakes in your air fryer's basket and cook at 375 degrees F for 10 minutes, flipping them halfway.
5. Serve them as an appetizer.
6. Enjoy!

Nutrition:
calories 212, fat 4, fiber 3, carbs 8, protein 10

Tomatoes Salsa

Preparation time: 10 minutes
Cooking time: 7 minutes
Servings: 6

Ingredients:
- 1 and ½ cups tomatoes, chopped
- 3 cups cucumber, chopped
- 1 teaspoons capers
- 1 garlic clove, minced
- 2 teaspoons lemon juice
- 1 tablespoon parsley, chopped
- 1 tablespoon basil, chopped
- Salt and black pepper to the taste

Directions:
1. In a pan that fits your air fryer, combine tomatoes with capers, garlic, lemon juice, parsley, salt and pepper, toss, introduce in the fryer, cook at 320 degrees F for 7 minutes, transfer to a bowl and cool the mixture down.
2. Add cucumbers and basil, toss, divide into small appetizer bowls and serve cold.
3. Enjoy!

Nutrition:
calories 161, fat 3, fiber 1, carbs 8, protein 12

Chard Party Spread

Preparation time: 10 minutes
Cooking time: 7 minutes
Servings: 4

Ingredients:
- 2 garlic cloves, minced
- 2 cup chard leaves
- ½ cup veggie stock
- ¼ cup sesame paste
- Salt and black pepper to the taste
- A drizzle of olive oil
- Juice of 1 lemon

Directions:
1. In a pan that fits your air fryer, mix stock with chard, salt and pepper, stir, introduce in the fryer and cook at 320 degrees F for 7 minutes.
2. Drain chard, transfer to your food processor, add garlic, sesame paste, lemon juice, olive oil and parsley, pulse well and divide into bowls and serve.
3. Enjoy!

Nutrition:
calories 202, fat 4, fiber 3, carbs 7, protein 8

Tomato and Bell Pepper Dip

Preparation time: 10 minutes
Cooking time: 10 minutes
Servings: 4

Ingredients:
- 1 tablespoon olive oil
- 1 cup yellow onion, chopped
- 2 garlic cloves, minced
- 2 cups sweet bell pepper, chopped
- ¼ cup sun-dried tomatoes, minced
- 2 tablespoons tomato paste
- ¼ cup veggie stock
- Salt and black pepper to the taste

Directions:
1. In a pan that fits your air fryer, combine oil with onion, garlic, bell pepper, tomatoes, tomato paste, stock, salt and pepper, toss, introduce in the fryer and cook at 365 degrees F for 10 minutes.
2. Stir, divide into bowls and serve.
3. Enjoy!

Nutrition:
calories 173, fat 4, fiber 3, carbs 7, protein 8

Corn Side Salad

Preparation time: 10 minutes
Cooking time: 10 minutes
Servings: 4

Ingredients:
- 3 cups corn
- A drizzle of olive oil
- Salt and black pepper to the taste
- 1 teaspoon sweet paprika
- 1 tablespoon stevia
- ½ teaspoon garlic powder
- ½ iceberg lettuce head, cut into medium strips
- ½ romaine lettuce head, cut into medium strips
- 1 cup canned black beans, drained
- 3 tablespoons cilantro, chopped
- 4 green onions, chopped
- 12 cherry tomatoes, sliced

Directions:
1. Put the corn in a pan that fits your air fryer, drizzle the oil, add salt, pepper, paprika, stevia and garlic powder, introduce in your air fryer and cook at 350 degrees F for 10 minutes.
2. Transfer corn to a salad bowl, add lettuce, black beans, tomatoes, green onions and cilantro, toss, divide between plates and serve as a side salad.
3. Enjoy!

Nutrition:
calories 162, fat 6, fiber 4, carbs 7, protein 6

Colored Veggie Mix

Preparation time: 10 minutes
Cooking time: 12 minutes
Servings: 6

Ingredients:
- 1 zucchini, sliced in half and roughly chopped
- 1 orange bell pepper, roughly chopped
- 1 green bell pepper, roughly chopped
- 1 red onion, roughly chopped
- 4 ounces brown mushrooms, halved
- Salt and black pepper to the taste
- 1 teaspoon Italian seasoning
- 1 cup cherry tomatoes, halved
- ½ cup kalamata olives, pitted and halved
- ¼ cup olive oil
- 3 tablespoons balsamic vinegar
- 2 tablespoons basil, chopped

Directions:
1. In a bowl, mix zucchini with mushrooms, orange bell pepper, green bell pepper, red onion, salt, pepper, Italian seasoning and oil, toss well, transfer to preheated air fryer at 380 degrees F and cook them for 12 minutes.
2. In a large bowl, combine mixed veggies with tomatoes, olives, vinegar and basil, toss, divide between plates and serve cold as a side dish.
3. Enjoy!

Nutrition:
calories 180, fat 5, fiber 8, carbs 10, protein 6

Leeks Medley

Preparation time: 10 minutes
Cooking time: 12 minutes
Servings: 4

Ingredients:

- 6 leeks, roughly chopped
- 1 tablespoon cumin, ground
- 1 tablespoon mint, chopped
- 1 tablespoon parsley, chopped
- 1 teaspoon garlic, minced
- A drizzle of olive oil
- Salt and black pepper to the taste

Directions:

1. In a pan that fits your air fryer, combine leeks with cumin, mint, parsley, garlic, salt, pepper and the oil, toss, introduce in your air fryer and cook at 350 degrees F for 12 minutes.
2. Divide leeks medley between plates and serve as a side dish.
3. Enjoy!

Nutrition:
calories 131, fat 7, fiber 3, carbs 10, protein 6

Corn and Tomatoes

Preparation time: 10 minutes
Cooking time: 13 minutes
Servings: 4

Ingredients:
- 2 cups corn
- 4 tomatoes, roughly chopped
- 1 tablespoon olive oil
- Salt and black pepper to the taste
- 1 tablespoon oregano, chopped
- 1 tablespoon parsley, chopped
- 2 tablespoons soft tofu, pressed and crumbled

Directions:
1. In a pan that fits your air fryer, combine corn with tomatoes, oil, salt, pepper, oregano and parsley, toss, introduce the pan in your air fryer and cook at 320 degrees F for 10 minutes.
2. Add tofu, toss, introduce in the fryer for 3 minutes more, divide between plates and serve as a side dish.
3. Enjoy!

Nutrition:
calories 171, fat 7, fiber 8, carbs 9, protein 6

Chapter 4 Poultry

Turkey and Parsley Pesto

Preparation time: 35 minutes

Cooking time: 35 minutes

Servings: 4

Ingredients:
- 1 cup parsley, chopped
- ½ cup olive oil
- ¼ cup red wine
- 4 garlic cloves
- A pinch of salt and black pepper
- A drizzle of maple syrup
- 2 turkey breasts, boneless, skinless and halved

Directions:
1. In a blender, mix the parsley, garlic, salt, pepper, oil, wine, and maple syrup; pulse to make a parsley pesto and then transfer to a bowl.
2. Add the turkey breasts to the bowl and toss well. Then place the bowl in the fridge for 30 minutes.
3. Drain the turkey breasts (retaining the parsley pesto), put them in your air fryer's basket and cook at 380 degrees F for 35 minutes, flipping the meat halfway.
4. Divide the turkey between plates, drizzle the parsley pesto, all over and serve.

Nutrition:
calories 274, fat 10, fiber 12, carbs 20, protein 17

Chicken Breasts and Veggies

Preparation time: 10 minutes
Cooking time: 20 minutes
Servings: 4

Ingredients:
- 2 pounds chicken breasts, skinless and boneless
- 2 tablespoons olive oil
- 1 red onion, chopped
- 2 garlic cloves, minced
- Salt and black pepper to taste
- 12 brown mushrooms, halved
- 1 red bell pepper, chopped
- 1 green bell pepper, roughly chopped
- 2 tablespoons cheddar cheese, shredded

Directions:
1. Season the chicken breasts with salt and pepper, and then rub with the garlic and 1 tablespoon of the oil.
2. Place the chicken breasts in your preheated air fryer's basket, cook at 390 degrees F for 6 minutes on each side, and divide between plates.
3. Heat up a pan with the remaining 1 tablespoon of the oil over medium heat; add the onions, stir, and cook for 2 minutes.
4. Add the mushrooms and bell peppers, stir, and cook for 5-6 minutes more.
5. Divide this next to the chicken, sprinkle the cheese all over, and serve.

Nutrition:
calories 285, fat 12, fiber 11, carbs 20, protein 22

Chicken and Green Coconut Sauce

Preparation time: 10 minutes
Cooking time: 16 minutes
Servings: 4

Ingredients:

- 10 green onions, roughly chopped
- 1 tablespoon ginger, grated
- 4 garlic cloves, minced
- 2 tablespoons oyster sauce
- 3 tablespoons soy sauce
- 1 teaspoon Chinese five spice
- 10 chicken drumsticks
- 1 cup coconut milk
- Salt and black pepper to taste
- 1 teaspoon olive oil
- ¼ cup parsley, chopped
- 1 tablespoon lemon juice

Directions:

1. In a blender, mix the green onions with the ginger, garlic, soy sauce, oyster sauce, five spice, salt, pepper, oil, and coconut milk; pulse well.
2. In a baking dish that fits your air fryer, mix the chicken with the green sauce, toss, and then place the dish in the air fryer.
3. Cook at 370 degrees F for 16 minutes, shaking the fryer once.
4. Divide between plates, sprinkle the parsley on top, drizzle the lemon juice all over, and serve.

Nutrition:
calories 281, fat 11, fiber 12, carbs 22, protein 16

Simple Chicken Thighs

Preparation time: 5 minutes
Cooking time: 16 minutes
Servings: 6

Ingredients:
- 8 chicken thighs
- 1 tablespoon turmeric powder
- 1 tablespoon coriander, ground
- 1 tablespoon ginger, grated
- 1 tablespoon sweet paprika
- Salt and black pepper to taste
- 2 tablespoons olive oil
- 1 tablespoon lime juice

Directions:
1. Place all the ingredients in a bowl and toss well.
2. Transfer the chicken thighs to your air fryer's basket and cook at 370 degrees F for 8 minutes on each side.
3. Divide between plates and serve with a side salad.

Nutrition:
calories 270, fat 11, fiber 11, carbs 17, protein 11

Chicken Breasts Delight

Preparation time: 5 minutes
Cooking time: 25 minutes
Servings: 6

Ingredients:
- 1 tablespoon olive oil
- 3½ pounds chicken breasts
- 1 cup chicken stock
- 1¼ cups yellow onion, chopped
- 1 tablespoon lime juice
- 2 teaspoons sweet paprika
- 1 teaspoon red pepper flakes
- 2 tablespoons green onions, chopped
- Salt and black pepper to taste

Directions:
1. Heat the oil up in a pan that fits your air fryer over medium heat.
2. Add the onions, lime juice, paprika, green onions, pepper flakes, salt, and pepper.
3. Stir the onion mixture and cook for 8 minutes.
4. Add the chicken and the stock, toss, and simmer for 1 more minute.
5. Transfer the pan to your air fryer and cook at 370 degrees F for 12 minutes.
6. Divide between plates and serve.

Nutrition:
calories 280, fat 11, fiber 13, carbs 27, protein 16

Tomato Chicken Mix

Preparation time: 10 minutes
Cooking time: 20 minutes
Servings: 6

Ingredients:

- 14 ounces tomato sauce
- 1 tablespoon olive oil
- 4 medium chicken breasts, skinless and boneless
- Salt and black pepper to taste
- 1 teaspoon oregano, dried
- 6 ounces mozzarella cheese, grated
- 1 teaspoon garlic powder

Directions:

1. Put the chicken in your air fryer and season with salt, pepper, garlic powder, and the oregano.
2. Cook the chicken at 360 degrees F for 5 minutes; then transfer to a pan that fits your air fryer, greased with the oil.
3. Add the tomato sauce, sprinkle the mozzarella on top, place the pan in the fryer, and cook at 350 degrees F for 15 minutes more.
4. Divide between plates and serve.

Nutrition:
calories 270, fat 10, fiber 16, carbs 16, protein 18

Chicken and Veggies

Preparation time: 10 minutes

Cooking time: 25 minutes

Servings: 4

Ingredients:
- 1 red onion, chopped
- 1 carrot, chopped
- 3 garlic cloves, minced
- 4 chicken breasts, boneless and skinless
- 1 celery stalk, chopped
- 1 cup chicken stock
- 2 tablespoons olive oil
- ½ teaspoon rosemary, dried
- 1 teaspoon sage, dried
- Salt and black pepper to taste

Directions:
1. In a pan that fits your air fryer, place all ingredients and toss well.
2. Put the pan in the fryer and cook at 360 degrees F for 25 minutes.
3. Divide everything between plates, serve, and enjoy!

Nutrition:
calories 292, fat 12, fiber 16, carbs 19, protein 15

Japanese Chicken Thighs

Preparation time: 10 minutes
Cooking time: 30 minutes
Servings: 5

Ingredients:
- 2 pounds chicken thighs
- Salt and black pepper to taste
- 5 spring onions, chopped
- 2 tablespoons olive oil
- 1 tablespoon sherry wine
- ½ teaspoon white vinegar
- 1 tablespoon soy sauce
- ¼ teaspoon sugar

Directions:
1. Season the chicken with salt and pepper, rub with 1 tablespoon of the oil, and put it in the air fryer's basket.
2. Cook at 360 degrees F for 10 minutes on each side and divide between plates.
3. Heat up a pan with the remaining tablespoon of oil over medium-high heat, and add the spring onions, sherry wine, vinegar, soy sauce, and sugar; whisk.
4. Cook for 10 minutes, drizzle over the chicken, and serve.

Nutrition:
calories 271, fat 8, fiber 12, carbs 26, protein 17

Air Fried Whole Chicken

Preparation time: 10 minutes

Cooking time: 20 minutes

Servings: 8

Ingredients:

- 1 whole chicken, cut into medium pieces
- 3 tablespoons white wine
- 2 carrots, chopped
- 1 cup chicken stock
- 1 tablespoon ginger, grated
- Salt and black pepper to taste

Directions:

1. In a pan that fits your air fryer, mix all of the ingredients.
2. Put the pan in the air fryer and cook at 370 degrees F for 20 minutes.
3. Divide between plates and serve.

Nutrition:

calories 220, fat 10, fiber 8, carbs 20, protein 16

Chicken Thighs and Rice

Preparation time: 5 minutes
Cooking time: 30 minutes
Servings: 4

Ingredients:

- 3 carrots, chopped
- 2 pounds chicken thighs, boneless and skinless
- ¼ cup red wine vinegar
- 4 garlic cloves, minced
- Salt and black pepper to taste
- 4 tablespoons olive oil
- 1 tablespoon garlic powder
- 1 tablespoon Italian seasoning
- 1 cup white rice
- 1 teaspoon turmeric powder
- 2 cups chicken stock

Directions:

1. In a pan that fits your air fryer, mix all of the ingredients and toss.
2. Place the pan in the fryer and cook at 370 degrees F for 30 minutes.
3. Divide between plates and serve.

Nutrition:

calories 280, fat 12, fiber 12, carbs 16, protein 13

Chapter5 Beef, Pork and Lamb

Beef Rolls

Preparation time: 10 minutes
Cooking time: 14 minutes
Servings: 4

Ingredients:
- 2 pounds beef steak, opened and flattened with a meat tenderizer
- Salt and black pepper to the taste
- 1 cup baby spinach
- 3 ounces red bell pepper, roasted and chopped
- 6 slices provolone cheese
- 3 tablespoons pesto

Directions:
1. Arrange flattened beef steak on a cutting board, spread pesto all over, add cheese in a single layer, add bell peppers, spinach, salt and pepper to the taste.
2. Roll your steak, secure with toothpicks, season again with salt and pepper, place roll in your air fryer's basket and cook at 400 degrees F for 14 minutes, rotating roll halfway.
3. Leave aside to cool down, cut into 2 inch smaller rolls, arrange on a platter and serve them as an appetizer.
4. Enjoy!

Nutrition:
calories 230, fat 1, fiber 3, carbs 12, protein 10

Greek Beef Meatballs Salad

Preparation time: 10 minutes
Cooking time: 10 minutes
Servings: 6

Ingredients:
- ¼ cup milk
- 17 ounces beef, ground
- 1 yellow onion, grated
- 5 bread slices, cubed
- 1 egg, whisked
- ¼ cup parsley, chopped
- Salt and black pepper to the taste
- 2 garlic cloves, minced
- ¼ cup mint, chopped
- 2 and ½ teaspoons oregano, dried
- 1 tablespoon olive oil
- Cooking spray
- 7 ounces cherry tomatoes, halved
- 1 cup baby spinach
- 1 and ½ tablespoons lemon juice
- 7 ounces Greek yogurt

Directions:
1. Put torn bread in a bowl, add milk, soak for a few minutes, squeeze and transfer to another bowl.
2. Add beef, egg, salt, pepper, oregano, mint, parsley, garlic and onion, stir and shape medium meatballs out of this mix.

3. Spray them with cooking spray, place them in your air fryer and cook at 370 degrees F for 10 minutes.
4. In a salad bowl, mix spinach with cucumber and tomato.
5. Add meatballs, the oil, some salt, pepper, lemon juice and yogurt, toss and serve.
6. Enjoy!

Nutrition:
calories 200, fat 4, fiber 8, carbs 13, protein 27

Beef Patties and Mushroom Sauce

Preparation time: 10 minutes
Cooking time: 25 minutes
Servings: 6

Ingredients:
- 2 pounds beef, ground
- Salt and black pepper to the taste
- ½ teaspoon garlic powder
- 1 tablespoon soy sauce
- ¼ cup beef stock
- ¾ cup flour
- 1 tablespoon parsley, chopped
- 1 tablespoon onion flakes
- For the sauce:
- 1 cup yellow onion, chopped
- 2 cups mushrooms, sliced
- 2 tablespoons bacon fat
- 2 tablespoons butter
- ½ teaspoon soy sauce
- ¼ cup sour cream
- ½ cup beef stock
- Salt and black pepper to the taste

Directions:
1. In a bowl, mix beef with salt, pepper, garlic powder, 1 tablespoon soy sauce, ¼ cup beef stock, flour, parsley and onion flakes, stir well, shape 6 patties, place them in your air fryer and cook at 350 degrees F for 14 minutes.

2. Meanwhile, heat up a pan with the butter and the bacon fat over medium heat, add mushrooms, stir and cook for 4 minutes.
3. Add onions, stir and cook for 4 minutes more.
4. Add ½ teaspoon soy sauce, sour cream and ½ cup stock, stir well, bring to a simmer and take off heat.
5. Divide beef patties on plates and serve with mushroom sauce on top.
6. Enjoy!

Nutrition:
calories 435, fat 23, fiber 4, carbs 6, protein 32

Beef Casserole

Preparation time: 30 minutes
Cooking time: 35 minutes
Servings: 12

Ingredients:
- 1 tablespoon olive oil
- 2 pounds beef, ground
- 2 cups eggplant, chopped
- Salt and black pepper to the taste
- 2 teaspoons mustard
- 2 teaspoons gluten free Worcestershire sauce
- 28 ounces canned tomatoes, chopped
- 2 cups mozzarella, grated
- 16 ounces tomato sauce
- 2 tablespoons parsley, chopped
- 1 teaspoon oregano, dried

Directions:
1. In a bowl, mix eggplant with salt, pepper and oil and toss to coat.
2. In another bowl, mix beef with salt, pepper, mustard and Worcestershire sauce, stir well and spread on the bottom of a pan that fits your air fryer.
3. Add eggplant mix, tomatoes, tomato sauce, parsley, oregano and sprinkle mozzarella at the end.
4. Introduce in your air fryer and cook at 360 degrees F for 35 minutes
5. Divide among plates and serve hot.
6. Enjoy!

Nutrition:
calories 200, fat 12, fiber 2, carbs 16, protein 15

Lamb and Spinach Mix

Preparation time: 10 minutes
Cooking time: 35 minutes
Servings: 6

Ingredients:
- 2 tablespoons ginger, grated
- 2 garlic cloves, minced
- 2 teaspoons cardamom, ground
- 1 red onion, chopped
- 1 pound lamb meat, cubed
- 2 teaspoons cumin powder
- 1 teaspoon garam masala
- ½ teaspoon chili powder
- 1 teaspoon turmeric
- 2 teaspoons coriander, ground
- 1 pound spinach
- 14 ounces canned tomatoes, chopped

Directions:
1. In a heat proof dish that fits your air fryer, mix lamb with spinach, tomatoes, ginger, garlic, onion, cardamom, cloves, cumin, garam masala, chili, turmeric and coriander, stir, introduce in preheated air fryer and cook at 360 degrees F for 35 minutes
2. Divide into bowls and serve.

3. Enjoy!

Nutrition:
calories 160, fat 6, fiber 3, carbs 17, protein 20

Lamb and Lemon Sauce

Preparation time: 10 minutes
Cooking time: 30 minutes
Servings: 4

Ingredients:
- 2 lamb shanks
- Salt and black pepper to the taste
- 2 garlic cloves, minced
- 4 tablespoons olive oil
- Juice from ½ lemon
- Zest from ½ lemon
- ½ teaspoon oregano, dried

Directions:
1. Season lamb with salt, pepper, rub with garlic, put in your air fryer and cook at 350 degrees F for 30 minutes.
2. Meanwhile, in a bowl, mix lemon juice with lemon zest, some salt and pepper, the olive oil and oregano and whisk very well.
3. Shred lamb, discard bone, divide among plates, drizzle the lemon dressing all over and serve.
4. Enjoy!

Nutrition:
calories 260, fat 7, fiber 3, carbs 15, protein 12

Lamb and Green Pesto

Preparation time: 1 hour
Cooking time: 45 minutes
Servings: 4

Ingredients:
- 1 cup parsley
- 1 cup mint
- 1 small yellow onion, roughly chopped
- 1/3 cup pistachios, chopped
- 1 teaspoon lemon zest, grated
- 5 tablespoons olive oil
- Salt and black pepper to the taste
- 2 pounds lamb riblets
- ½ onion, chopped
- 5 garlic cloves, minced
- Juice from 1 orange

Directions:
1. In your food processor, mix parsley with mint, onion, pistachios, lemon zest, salt, pepper and oil and blend very well.
2. Rub lamb with this mix, place in a bowl, cover and leave in the fridge for 1 hour.
3. Transfer lamb to a baking dish that fits your air fryer, also add garlic, drizzle orange juice and cook in your air fryer at 300 degrees F for 45 minutes.
4. Divide lamb on plates and serve.
5. Enjoy!

Nutrition:
calories 200, fat 4, fiber 6, carbs 15, protein 7

Lamb and Lemon Sauce Recipe

Preparation time: 40 Minutes
Servings: 4

Ingredients:
- 2 lamb shanks
- 2 garlic cloves; minced
- 4 tbsp. olive oil
- Juice from 1/2 lemon
- Zest from 1/2 lemon
- 1/2 tsp. oregano; dried
- Salt and black pepper to the taste

Directions:
1. Season lamb with salt, pepper, rub with garlic, put in your air fryer and cook at 350 °F, for 30 minutes.
2. Meanwhile; in a bowl, mix lemon juice with lemon zest, some salt and pepper, the olive oil and oregano and whisk very well. Shred lamb, discard bone, divide among plates, drizzle the lemon dressing all over and serve.

Nutrition:
Calories: 260; Fat: 7; Fiber: 3; Carbs: 15; Protein: 12

Provencal Pork Recipe

Preparation time: 25 Minutes
Servings: 2

Ingredients:

- 7 oz. pork tenderloin
- 1 red onion; sliced
- 1 yellow bell pepper; cut into strips
- 2 tsp. Provencal herbs
- 1/2 tbsp. mustard
- 1 tbsp. olive oil
- 1 green bell pepper; cut into strips
- Salt and black pepper to the taste

Directions:

1. In a baking dish that fits your air fryer, mix yellow bell pepper with green bell pepper, onion, salt, pepper, Provencal herbs and half of the oil and toss well.
2. Season pork with salt, pepper, mustard and the rest of the oil, toss well and add to veggies. Introduce everything in your air fryer,
3. Cook at 370 °F, for 15 minutes; divide among plates and serve.

Nutrition:

Calories: 300; Fat: 8; Fiber: 7; Carbs: 21; Protein: 23

Lemony Lamb Leg Recipe

Preparation time: 1 hour 10 Minutes
Servings: 6

Ingredients:

- 4 lbs. lamb leg
- 2 tbsp. olive oil
- 2 springs rosemary; chopped.
- 2 tbsp. lemon juice
- 2 lbs. baby potatoes
- 1 cup beef stock
- 2 tbsp. parsley; chopped
- 2 tbsp. oregano; chopped
- 1 tbsp. lemon rind; grated
- 3 garlic cloves; minced
- Salt and black pepper to the taste

Directions:

1. Make small cuts all over lamb, insert rosemary springs and season with salt and pepper.
2. In a bowl; mix 1 tbsp. oil with oregano, parsley, garlic, lemon juice and rind; stir and rub lamb with this mix.
3. Heat up a pan that fits your air fryer with the rest of the oil over medium high heat, add potatoes; stir and cook for 3 minutes.
4. Add lamb and stock; stir, introduce in your air fryer and cook at 360 °F, for 1 hour. Divide everything on plates and serve.

Nutrition:

Calories: 264; Fat: 4; Fiber: 12; Carbs: 27; Protein: 32

Beef Roast and Wine Sauce Recipe

Preparation time: 55 Minutes
Servings: 6

Ingredients:

- 3 lbs. beef roast
- 17 oz. beef stock
- 4 garlic cloves; minced
- 3 carrots; chopped
- 5 potatoes; chopped
- 3 oz. red wine
- 1/2 tsp. chicken salt
- Salt and black pepper to the taste
- 1/2 tsp. smoked paprika
- 1 yellow onion; chopped

Directions:

1. In a bowl; mix salt, pepper, chicken salt and paprika; stir, rub beef with this mix and put it in a big pan that fits your air fryer.
2. Add onion, garlic, stock, wine, potatoes and carrots, introduce in your air fryer and cook at 360 °F, for 45 minutes. Divide everything on plates and serve.

Nutrition:
Calories: 304; Fat: 20; Fiber: 7; Carbs: 20; Protein: 32

Fennel Flavored Pork Roast Recipe

Preparation time: 1 hour 10 Minutes
Servings: 10

Ingredients:

- 5 ½ lbs. pork loin roast; trimmed
- 1 tbsp. fennel seeds
- 2 tsp. red pepper; crushed
- 1/4 cup olive oil
- 3 garlic cloves; minced
- 2 tbsp. rosemary; chopped.
- 1 tsp. fennel; ground
- Salt and black pepper to the taste

Directions:

1. In your food processor mix garlic with fennel seeds, fennel, rosemary, red pepper, some black pepper and the olive oil and blend until you obtain a paste.
2. Spread 2 tbsp. garlic paste on pork loin, rub well, season with salt and pepper, introduce in your preheated air fryer and cook at 350 °F, for 30 minutes.
3. Reduce heat to 300 °F and cook for 15 minutes more. Slice pork, divide among plates and serve.

Nutrition:

Calories: 300; Fat: 14; Fiber: 9; Carbs: 26; Protein: 22

Stuffed Pork Steaks

Preparation time: 10 minutes
Cooking time: 20 minutes
Servings: 4

Ingredients:
- Zest from 2 limes, grated
- Zest from 1 orange, grated
- Juice from 1 orange
- Juice from 2 limes
- 4 teaspoons garlic, minced
- ¾ cup olive oil
- 1 cup cilantro, chopped
- 1 cup mint, chopped
- 1 teaspoon oregano, dried
- Salt and black pepper to the taste
- 2 teaspoons cumin, ground
- 4 pork loin steaks
- 2 pickles, chopped
- 4 ham slices
- 6 Swiss cheese slices
- 2 tablespoons mustard

Directions:
1. In your food processor, mix lime zest and juice with orange zest and juice, garlic, oil, cilantro, mint, oregano, cumin, salt and pepper and blend well.

2. Season steaks with salt and pepper, place them into a bowl, add marinade and toss to coat.
3. Place steaks on a working surface, divide pickles, cheese, mustard and ham on them, roll and secure with toothpicks.
4. Put stuffed pork steaks in your air fryer and cook at 340 degrees F for 20 minutes.
5. Divide among plates and serve with a side salad.
6. Enjoy!

Nutrition:
calories 270, fat 7, fiber 2, carbs 13, protein 20

Pork Chops and Mushrooms Mix

Preparation time: 10 minutes
Cooking time: 40 minutes
Servings: 3

Ingredients:

- 8 ounces mushrooms, sliced
- 1 teaspoon garlic powder
- 1 yellow onion, chopped
- 1 cup mayonnaise
- 3 pork chops, boneless
- 1 teaspoon nutmeg
- 1 tablespoon balsamic vinegar
- ½ cup olive oil

Directions:

1. Heat up a pan that fits your air fryer with the oil over medium heat, add mushrooms and onions, stir and cook for 4 minutes.
2. Add pork chops, nutmeg and garlic powder and brown on both sides.
3. Introduce pan your air fryer at 330 degrees F and cook for 30 minutes.
4. Add vinegar and mayo, stir, divide everything on plates and serve.
5. Enjoy!

Nutrition:
calories 600, fat 10, fiber 1, carbs 8, protein 30

Beef Stuffed Squash

Preparation time: 10 minutes
Cooking time: 40 minutes
Servings: 2

Ingredients:
- 1 spaghetti squash, pricked
- 1 pound beef, ground
- Salt and black pepper to the taste
- 3 garlic cloves, minced
- 1 yellow onion, chopped
- 1 Portobello mushroom, sliced
- 28 ounces canned tomatoes, chopped
- 1 teaspoon oregano, dried
- ¼ teaspoon cayenne pepper
- ½ teaspoon thyme, dried
- 1 green bell pepper, chopped

Directions:
1. Put spaghetti squash in your air fryer, cook at 350 degrees F for 20 minutes, transfer to a cutting board, and cut into halves and discard seeds.

2. Heat up a pan over medium high heat, add meat, garlic, onion and mushroom, stir and cook until meat browns.
3. Add salt, pepper, thyme, oregano, cayenne, tomatoes and green pepper, stir and cook for 10 minutes.
4. Stuff squash with this beef mix, introduce in the fryer and cook at 360 degrees F for 10 minutes.
5. Divide among plates and serve.
6. Enjoy!

Nutrition:
calories 260, fat 7, fiber 2, carbs 14, protein 10

Chapter6 Vegan and Vegetarian

Cajun Asparagus

Preparation time: 5 minutes

Cooking time: 5 minutes

Servings: 4

Ingredients:
- 1 teaspoon extra virgin olive oil
- 1 bunch asparagus, trimmed
- ½ tablespoon Cajun seasoning

Directions:
1. In a bowl, mix the asparagus with the oil and Cajun seasoning; coat the asparagus well.
2. Put the asparagus in your air fryer and cook at 400 degrees F for 5 minutes.
3. Divide between plates and serve.

Nutrition:
calories 151, fat 3, fiber 4, carbs 9, protein 4

Squash Salad

Preparation time: 5 minutes
Cooking time: 12 minutes
Servings: 4

Ingredients:

- 1 butternut squash, cubed
- 2 tablespoons balsamic vinegar
- 1 bunch cilantro, chopped
- Salt and black pepper to taste
- 1 tablespoon olive oil

Directions:

1. Put the squash in your air fryer, and add the salt, pepper, and oil; toss well.
2. Cook at 400 degrees F for 12 minutes.
3. Transfer the squash to a bowl, add the vinegar and cilantro, and toss.
4. Serve and enjoy!

Nutrition:

calories 151, fat 4, fiber 7, carbs 11, protein 8

Creamy Squash Mix

Preparation time: 5 minutes
Cooking time: 12 minutes
Servings: 6

Ingredients:
- 1 big butternut squash, roughly cubed
- 1 cup sour cream
- Salt and black pepper to taste
- 1 tablespoon parsley, chopped
- A drizzle of olive oil

Directions:
1. Put the squash in your air fryer, add the salt and pepper, and rub with the oil.
2. Cook at 400 degrees F for 12 minutes.
3. Transfer the squash to a bowl, and add the cream and the parsley.
4. Toss and serve.

Nutrition:
calories 200, fat 7, fiber 6, carbs 11, protein 7

Orange Carrots

Preparation time: 5 minutes
Cooking time: 15 minutes
Servings: 4

Ingredients:
- 1½ pounds baby carrots
- 2 teaspoons orange zest
- 2 tablespoons cider vinegar
- ½ cup orange juice
- A handful of parsley, chopped
- A drizzle of olive oil

Directions:
1. Put the baby carrots in your air fryer's basket, add the orange zest and oil, and rub the carrots well.
2. Cook at 350 degrees F for 15 minutes.
3. Transfer the carrots to a bowl, and then add the vinegar, orange juice, and parsley.
4. Toss, serve, and enjoy!

Nutrition:
calories 151, fat 6, fiber 6, carbs 11, protein 5

Tomato Salad

Preparation time: 5 minutes
Cooking time: 5 minutes
Servings: 8

Ingredients:

- 1 red onion, sliced
- 2 ounces feta cheese, crumbled
- Salt and black pepper to taste
- 1 pint mixed cherry tomatoes, halved
- 2 ounces pecans
- 2 tablespoons olive oil

Directions:

1. In your air fryer, mix the tomatoes with the salt, pepper, onions, and the oil.
2. Cook at 400 degrees F for 5 minutes.
3. Transfer to a bowl and add the pecans and the cheese.
4. Toss and serve.

Nutrition:
calories 151, fat 4, fiber 6, carbs 9, protein 4

Tomato and Green Beans Salad

Preparation time: 5 minutes
Cooking time: 6 minutes
Servings: 4

Ingredients:
- 1 pound green beans, trimmed and halved
- 2 green onions, chopped
- 5 ounces canned green chilies, chopped
- 1 jalapeno pepper, chopped
- A drizzle of olive oil
- 2 teaspoons chili powder
- 1 teaspoon garlic powder
- Salt and black pepper to taste
- 8 cherry tomatoes, halved

Directions:
1. Place all ingredients in a pan that fits your air fryer, and mix / toss.
2. Put the pan in the fryer and cook at 400 degrees F for 6 minutes.
3. Divide the mix between plates and serve hot.

Nutrition:
calories 200, fat 4, fiber 7, carbs 12, protein 6

Bell Peppers and Kale

Preparation time: 5 minutes
Cooking time: 15 minutes
Servings: 4

Ingredients:
- 2 red bell peppers, cut into strips
- 2 green bell peppers, cut into strips
- ½ pound kale leaves
- Salt and black pepper to taste
- 2 yellow onions, roughly chopped
- ¼ cup veggie stock
- 2 tablespoons tomato sauce

Directions:
1. Add all ingredients to a pan that fits your air fryer; mix well.
2. Place the pan in the fryer and cook at 360 degrees F for 15 minutes.
3. Divide between plates, serve, and enjoy!

Nutrition:
calories 161, fat 7, fiber 6, carbs 12, protein 7

Garlic Parsnips

Preparation time: 5 minutes
Cooking time: 15 minutes
Servings: 4

Ingredients:
- 1 pound parsnips, cut into chunks
- 1 tablespoon olive oil
- 6 garlic cloves, minced
- 1 tablespoon balsamic vinegar
- Salt and black pepper to taste

Directions:
1. Add all of the ingredients to a bowl and mix well.
2. Place them in the air fryer and cook at 380 degrees F for 15 minutes.
3. Divide between plates and serve.

Nutrition:
calories 121, fat 3, fiber 6, carbs 12, protein 6

Broccoli and Pomegranate

Preparation time: 5 minutes

Cooking time: 7 minutes

Servings: 4

Ingredients:

- 1 broccoli head, florets separated
- Salt and black pepper to taste
- 1 pomegranate, seeds separated
- A drizzle of olive oil

Directions:

1. In a bowl, mix the broccoli with the salt, pepper, and oil; toss.
2. Put the florets in your air fryer and cook at 400 degrees F for 7 minutes.
3. Divide between plates, sprinkle the pomegranate seeds all over, and serve.

Nutrition:

calories 141, fat 3, fiber 4, carbs 11, protein 4

Bacon Cauliflower

Preparation time: 5 minutes
Cooking time: 12 minutes
Servings: 4

Ingredients:
- 1 cauliflower head, florets separated
- 1 tablespoon olive oil
- Salt and black pepper to taste
- ½ cup bacon, cooked and chopped
- 2 tablespoons dill, chopped

Directions:
1. Put the cauliflower in your air fryer and add the salt, pepper, and oil; toss well.
2. Cook at 400 degrees F for 12 minutes.
3. Divide the cauliflower between plates, sprinkle the bacon and the dill on top, and serve.

Nutrition:
calories 200, fat 7, fiber 5, carbs 17, protein 7

Chapter7 Desserts

Crispy Apples Recipe

Preparation time: 20 Minutes
Servings: 4

Ingredients:

- 2 tsp. cinnamon powder
- 5 apples; cored and cut into chunks
- 4 tbsp. butter
- 1/4 cup flour
- 3/4 cup old fashioned rolled oats
- 1/2 tsp. nutmeg powder
- 1 tbsp. maple syrup
- 1/2 cup water
- 1/4 cup brown sugar

Directions:

1. Put the apples in a pan that fits your air fryer, add cinnamon, nutmeg, maple syrup and water
2. In a bowl; mix butter with oats, sugar, salt and flour; stir, drop spoonfuls of this mix on top of apples, introduce in your air fryer and cook at 350 °F, for 10 minutes. Serve warm.

Nutrition:

Calories: 200; Fat: 6; Fiber: 8; Carbs: 29; Protein: 12

Chocolate Cookies Recipe

Preparation time: 35 Minutes
Servings: 12

Ingredients:

- 1 tsp. vanilla extract
- 2 cups flour
- 1/2 cup butter
- 1 egg
- 4 tbsp. sugar
- 1/2 cup unsweetened chocolate chips

Directions:

1. Heat up a pan with the butter over medium heat; stir and cook for 1 minute
2. In a bowl; mix egg with vanilla extract and sugar and stir well
3. Add melted butter, flour and half of the chocolate chips and stir everything.
4. Transfer this to a pan that fits your air fryer, spread the rest of the chocolate chips on top, introduce in the fryer at 330 °F and bake for 25 minutes. Slice when it's cold and serve

Nutrition:

Calories: 230; Fat: 12; Fiber: 2; Carbs: 4; Protein: 5

Lentils and Dates Brownies Recipe

Preparation time: 25 Minutes
Servings: 8

Ingredients:
- 28 oz. canned lentils; rinsed and drained
- 1/2 tsp. baking soda
- 4 tbsp. almond butter
- 12 dates
- 1 tbsp. honey
- 1 banana; peeled and chopped.
- 2 tbsp. cocoa powder

Directions:
1. In your food processor, mix lentils with butter, banana, cocoa, baking soda and honey and blend really well.
2. Add dates, pulse a few more times, pour this into a greased pan that fits your air fryer, spread evenly, introduce in the fryer at 360 °F and bake for 15 minutes.
3. Take brownies mix out of the oven, cut, arrange on a platter and serve

Nutrition:
Calories: 162; Fat: 4; Fiber: 2; Carbs: 3; Protein: 4

Strawberry Shortcakes Recipe

Preparation time: 65 Minutes
Servings: 6

Ingredients:
- 1/4 cup sugar+ 4 tbsp.
- 1 ½ cup flour
- 1 tsp. baking powder
- 1 tbsp. mint; chopped
- 1 tsp. lime zest; grated
- 1/4 tsp. baking soda
- 1/3 cup butter
- 1 cup buttermilk
- 1 egg; whisked
- 2 cups strawberries; sliced
- Cooking spray
- 1 tbsp. rum
- 1/2 cup whipping cream

Directions:
1. In a bowl; mix flour with 1/4 cup sugar, baking powder and baking soda and stir
2. In another bowl, mix buttermilk with egg; stir, add to flour mix and whisk.
3. Spoon this dough into 6 jars greased with cooking spray, cover with tin foil, arrange them in your air fryer cook at 360 °F, for 45 minutes

4. Meanwhile; in a bowl, mix strawberries with 3 tbsp. sugar, rum, mint and lime zest; stir and leave aside in a cold place
5. In another bowl, mix whipping cream with 1 tbsp. sugar and stir. Take jars out, divide strawberry mix and whipped cream on top and serve.

Nutrition:

Calories: 164; Fat: 2; Fiber: 3; Carbs: 5; Protein: 2

Cocoa Cookies Recipe

Preparation time: 24 Minutes
Servings: 12

Ingredients:
- 6 oz. coconut oil; melted
- 6 eggs
- 1/2 tsp. baking powder
- 4 oz. cream cheese
- 3 oz. cocoa powder
- 2 tsp. vanilla
- 5 tbsp. sugar

Directions:
1. In a blender, mix eggs with coconut oil, cocoa powder, baking powder, vanilla, cream cheese and swerve and stir using a mixer
2. Pour this into a lined baking dish that fits your air fryer, introduce in the fryer at 320 °F and bake for 14 minutes. Slice cookie sheet into rectangles and serve

Nutrition:
Calories: 178; Fat: 14; Fiber: 2; Carbs: 3; Protein: 5

Mini Lava Cakes Recipe

Preparation time: 30 Minutes
Servings: 3

Ingredients:

- 1 egg
- 4 tbsp. sugar
- 2 tbsp. olive oil
- 1 tbsp. cocoa powder
- 1/2 tsp. baking powder
- 4 tbsp. milk
- 4 tbsp. flour
- 1/2 tsp. orange zest

Directions:

1. In a bowl; mix egg with sugar, oil, milk, flour, salt, cocoa powder, baking powder and orange zest; stir very well and pour this into greased ramekins
2. Add ramekins to your air fryer and cook at 320 °F, for 20 minutes. Serve lava cakes warm.

Nutrition:

Calories: 201; Fat: 7; Fiber: 8; Carbs: 23; Protein: 4

Lime Cheesecake Recipe

Preparation time: 4 hours and 14 minutes
Servings: 10

Ingredients:
- 2 tbsp. butter; melted
- 4 oz. flour
- 1/4 cup coconut; shredded
- 2 tsp. sugar

For the filling:
- 1 lb. cream cheese
- Juice form 1 lime
- 2 cups hot water
- Zest from 1 lime; grated
- 2 sachets lime jelly

Directions:
1. In a bowl; mix coconut with flour, butter and sugar; stir well and press this on the bottom of a pan that fits your air fryer
2. Meanwhile; put the hot water in a bowl, add jelly sachets and stir until it dissolves.
3. Put cream cheese in a bowl, add jelly, lime juice and zest and whisk really well
4. Add this over the crust, spread, introduce in the air fryer and cook at 300 °F, for 4 minutes. Keep in the fridge for 4 hours before serving.

Nutrition:
Calories: 260; Fat: 23; Fiber: 2; Carbs: 5; Protein: 7

Plum Cake Recipe

Preparation time: 1 hour and 20 Minutes
Servings: 8

Ingredients:

- 1 ¾ lbs. plums; pitted and cut into quarters
- 1 package dried yeast
- 7 oz. flour
- 5 tbsp. sugar
- 3 oz. warm milk
- 1 oz. butter; soft
- 1 egg; whisked
- Zest from 1 lemon; grated
- 1 oz. almond flakes

Directions:

1. In a bowl; mix yeast with butter, flour and 3 tbsp. sugar and stir well
2. Add milk and egg and whisk for 4 minutes until you obtain a dough
3. Arrange the dough in a spring form pan that fits your air fryer and which you've greased with some butter, cover and leave aside for 1 hour. Arrange plumps on top of the butter, sprinkle the rest of the sugar, introduce in your air fryer at 350 degrees F, bake for 36 minutes; cool down, sprinkle almond flakes and lemon zest on top, slice and serve.

Nutrition:

Calories: 192; Fat: 4; Fiber: 2; Carbs: 6; Protein: 7

Ginger Cheesecake Recipe

Preparation time: 2 hours and 30 Minutes
Servings: 6

Ingredients:
- 2 tsp. butter; melted
- 1/2 cup ginger cookies; crumbled
- 16 oz. cream cheese; soft
- 1/2 tsp. vanilla extract
- 1/2 tsp. nutmeg; ground
- 2 eggs
- 1/2 cup sugar
- 1 tsp. rum

Directions:
1. Grease a pan with the butter and spread cookie crumbs on the bottom
2. In a bowl; beat cream cheese with nutmeg, vanilla, rum and eggs, whisk well and spread over the cookie crumbs.
3. Introduce in your air fryer and cook at 340 °F, for 20 minutes. Leave cheesecake to cool down and keep in the fridge for 2 hours before slicing and serving it

Nutrition:
Calories: 412; Fat: 12; Fiber: 6; Carbs: 20; Protein: 6

Cocoa and Almond Bars Recipe

Preparation time: 34 Minutes
Servings: 6

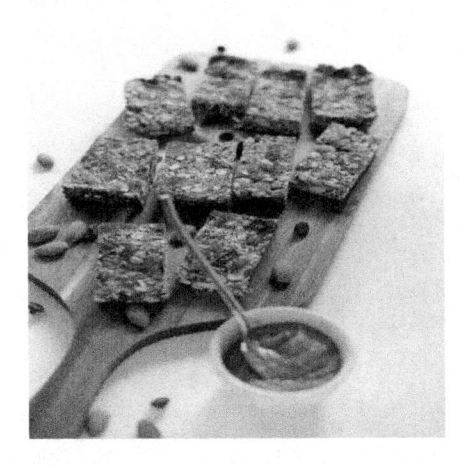

Ingredients:

- 1/4 cup cocoa nibs
- 1 cup almonds; soaked and drained
- 1/4 cup coconut; shredded
- 8 dates; pitted and soaked
- 2 tbsp. cocoa powder
- 1/4 cup hemp seeds
- 1/4 cup goji berries

Directions:

1. Put almonds in your food processor, blend, add hemp seeds, cocoa nibs, cocoa powder, goji, coconut and blend very well
2. Add dates, blend well again, spread on a lined baking sheet that fits your air fryer and cook at 320 °F, for 4 minutes. Cut into equal parts and keep in the fridge for 30 minutes before serving.

Nutrition:

Calories: 140; Fat: 6; Fiber: 3; Carbs: 7; Protein: 19

Conclusion

With a revolutionary kitchen appliance like the air fryer, cooking easy, healthy and delicious meals at home has become more practical. Not only will you be saving time but more importantly, you'll be cutting back on oil in your food.

Just remember that a little goes a long way. Once you get in the habit of air frying your foods, you'll never return to traditional pan or deep frying ever again.

Your body will thank you for cooking food the best way possible.

We hope with this cookbook you were able to explore further the power of the air fryer in preparing a variety of dishes. You now have discovered a whole new world of cooking via rapidly circulating hot air instead of hot oil. The air fryer is simply the perfect companion for any home cook who wants to create dishes that are nutritious and quick to prepare.

Now go ahead and enjoy cooking happy air frying!

Made in the USA
Middletown, DE
11 September 2019